THE PORT OF LIVERPOOL IN THE 1960s AND 1970s

Ian Collard

AMBERLEY

First published 2018

Amberley Publishing
The Hill, Stroud, Gloucestershire, GL5 4EP
www.amberley-books.com

Copyright © Ian Collard, 2018

The right of Ian Collard to be identified as the
Author of this work has been asserted in accordance with
the Copyrights, Designs and Patents Act 1988.

ISBN 978 1 4456 8141 2 (print)
ISBN 978 1 4456 8142 9 (ebook)

British Library Cataloguing in Publication Data.
A catalogue record for this book is available from the
British Library.

Origination by Amberley Publishing.
Printed in Great Britain.

Introduction

The 1960s and 1970s were a period of change and transition for the Port of Liverpool. By the end of the '60s the container revolution was gaining momentum and other ports were beginning to equip themselves with container handling facilities. The new Royal Seaforth Dock was opened to provide for the transportation of container traffic, grain and timber products. It was at this time that the number of passengers travelling by air was increasing and the passenger liners were being taken out of service and sold. The landing stage at Liverpool was scrapped in 1975/76 and a new stage for the Isle of Man Steam Packet and the Mersey ferries was opened.

In the early eighteenth century an Act of Parliament was passed entitled 'An Act for making a convenient Dock or Basin, at Liverpool, for the security of all ships trading to and from the Port of Liverpool'. The dock was opened in 1715, and it was the first enclosed commercial dock to ever be built and Liverpool was looked upon as the pioneer in dock construction. South Dock, later known as Salthouse Dock, was opened in 1753 and George's Dock was completed in 1771. Lighthouses were built and dues levied on all vessels were brought under the control of Dock Trustees appointed by Liverpool Town Council. Commercial traffic increased dramatically during the American War of Independence and King's, Queen's, Prince's and Coburg Docks were all built. The new Custom House was completed in 1839 and Brunswick Dock was opened in 1832 for the timber trade. Waterloo, Clarence and Victoria Docks were built for the coastal trade and the famous Albert Dock and warehouses were completed in 1846, being officially opened by Prince Albert.

A Royal Commission was appointed in 1853 to investigate complaints by merchants and it recommended that a new body be formed to take over the running of the docks. A Bill was introduced in Parliament in 1857 and after a long and expensive struggle it was passed by both Houses. The Bill created the Mersey Docks & Harbour Board, who assumed responsibility for the dock system from 1 January 1858 and this body would be controlled by twenty-eight Dock Trustees. John Laird was appointed as a nominee of the Government.

From its creation, the Board and the Mersey Dock Company were responsible for fostering trade, developing docks, conserving the river and pilotage, which had been under the control and guidance of the twenty-eight Dock Trustee members, twenty-four of whom were elected by those who paid the rates and dues on ships and goods coming in and leaving the port. The remaining four members were nominated by the Government.

The new Board held its first meeting on 5 January 1858 and needed to look at the creation of more dock accommodation for the increasing trade passing through the port. The previous twenty-five years had seen tonnage passing through the port increase from 1,540,057 tons to 4,645,362 tons and larger and longer steamships entering the dock system. On the Liverpool side of the river the Canadian timber trade had increased so rapidly that the berths at Brunswick Dock had become completely inadequate and vessels were being delayed for an average of thirty days.

There were also problems over the inadequate depth of water at the dock entrances and some large, modern vessels could not enter the system. In the first six months of 1857, 112 vessels had been held up in the river through lack of sufficient depth of water, and 225 were delayed through a shortage of berthing space. The new Board came to the conclusion that the work already began at Birkenhead should be completed but objectors said that the Birkenhead Docks were like 'a shop on the wrong side of the street'. In 1858 the revenue raised on goods and shipping amounted to £457,299 and the dock estate covered an area of 1,400 acres. Foreign imports passing through the port amounted to 1,100,000 tons and goods exported were almost double that figure. The exports were valued at £50,889,668 and imports were around the same amount.

Morpeth and Alfred Docks were extended and the Great Float opened in 1866. The entrance to the docks was through Alfred Basin and the engineers experienced problems keeping this dock free of sand and silt. After much experimentation, new entrances were built at Alfred Dock, which were opened by HRH the

Duke of Edinburgh on 21 June 1866. Most of the quays on the Birkenhead Dock Estate were served by an extensive system of railway lines, which were connected to a large distribution depot at Morpeth Dock.

The first work the Mersey Docks & Harbour Board undertook was to build Canning Dock for the timber trade and to construct the Herculaneum Graving Docks. In 1873 a further Act of Parliament was passed to enable the Board to spend £4 million to construct Langton, Alexandra and Hornby Docks, which created improved facilities for larger vessels entering the port. A further £3 million was spent on deep-water berths at Langton and Canada Docks and a new graving dock was opened at Canada Dock.

Facilities to allow passenger vessels to berth were built at Liverpool Pier Head. The northern section was known as the Prince's Landing Stage and in 1874 the Georges Stage, used by the ferries was joined together with the Prince's Stage and extended. However, prior to it being opened to the public it was almost destroyed by fire. It was rebuilt and the new stage was opened in 1876. Since then the stage was modified and extended to measure 2,534 feet long by 80 feet wide, becoming able to carry approximately 200 pontoons. There were ten bridges connecting with the shore and the 550-foot-long floating roadway gave access to private and commercial vehicles. Riverside railway station opened in 1895 to enable passengers from the steamers to get to their destinations more quickly and easily than having to be transported to the other major railway stations in the city. Both stages were scrapped in 1975/76, when the passenger liners ceased to operate from Liverpool and a new stage for the Mersey ferries and the Isle of Man Steam Packet was constructed and opened in 1975.

In 1878 the Foreign Animals Wharves were established at Wallasey and Woodside and came to handle an average of 500,000 animals a year. Cattle were shipped onwards or were slaughtered at the lairage and chilled meat was sent on from the wharf. Cattle were imported, mostly from Ireland, and were inspected by Ministry of Agriculture veterinary officers for disease and fitness to travel from the docks. The ships from Ireland arrived at Woodside or the Wallasey Stage most mornings and cattle were herded up the special bridges to the lairage at Morpeth Dock.

The Liverpool Overhead Railway was opened in 1893 and ran between Herculaneum Dock and Alexandra Dock in the north. The following year it was extended to Seaforth, Waterloo and Dingle in the south of the city. Land was purchased at Wallasey for oil storage.

In 1900 the water was run out of George's Dock for the Mersey Docks & Harbour Board to build their new headquarters. The Royal Liver Building and Cunard Building were later built to the north of the site. An Act of Parliament of 1906 allowed the Board to construct the Gladstone Graving Dock, which was opened by King George V and Queen Mary on 11 July 1913. The whole project was completed in 1927 and at the time the system contained the largest and deepest docks in the world.

The electrification of the dock system was completed in 1925. Electrical energy was supplied at high pressure and was distributed for power and lighting purposes. Approximately 81 miles of main cable was laid and the Clarence Dock power station, which also generated electricity for parts of Lancashire and Cheshire, supplied the power. Electrically operated bridges were built and Bidston Dock was completed in 1933.

In the late 1950s and 1960s several of the berths at Birkenhead Docks were rebuilt, old warehouses were demolished and new sheds were constructed. The Vittoria Dock loading berths were completely redesigned and modern warehouses were built for Clan Line and Alfred Holt & Company Limited. The Tranmere Oil Terminal was opened in 1960 to cater for the growing oil trade into the Port of Liverpool. Prior to this, petroleum, fuel oil and other refined products were discharged at the Dingle Tanker Buoy Berth, where four floating moorings could accommodate tankers up to 18,000 tons deadweight. The terminal had six submarine pipelines that were connected to shore tanks. This provided the oil companies with a storage capacity of 402,176 tons and five tanks provided by the Mersey Docks & Harbour Company with a capacity of 12,500 tons. Crude oil is pumped ashore at Tranmere and is transferred through a 15-mile pipeline to storage facilities at Stanlow in Cheshire. The Stanlow Refinery is part of the Shell Stanlow Manufacturing Complex and is situated at Ellesmere Port in Cheshire.

By the early 1960s the transportation of goods in containers was gaining momentum and the large shipping companies were discussing plans to build purpose-built container ships. In 1964 the Mersey Docks & Harbour Board commissioned a feasibility report on building a deep-water extension to the port to accommodate the new, larger container vessels. When completed, the Royal Seaforth Dock contained special berths for meat and packaged timber, a grain terminal and deepwater container berths, all incorporated within the new dock system. The four container berths are each 900 feet long and have large cranes to lift the containers on and off the vessels. There is also room to store and stack the containers as 60 acres of land are allocated for this purpose. A special meat terminal was incorporated in the scheme and this is able to handle the largest refrigerated ships in service. Elevators unload the meat and convey it to a cold store transit facility, or delivery can also be made directly to refrigerated vehicles on the quayside.

One of the main aspects of the new terminal that would clearly affect Birkenhead Docks was the provision of a giant grain terminal with a capacity of 100,000 tons. The largest bulk carriers afloat can berth alongside, and the vessels are unloaded at a rate of 2,000 tons an hour. The grain is fed directly from the silo to a gallery, where vehicles are loaded simultaneously. The new dock at Seaforth also provided specialist facilities for the unloading of packaged timber.

The Mersey Docks & Harbour Company was established in 1971, which freed the old Board of many of its responsibilities and obligations. The new Royal Seaforth Dock was opened by Her Royal Highness the Princess Anne that year and this was to have a dramatic effect on the fortunes of the other sectors of the dock system. The 3 miles of docks to the south of Liverpool Pier Head were closed to shipping in 1972 as it was felt that their water was too shallow and that the narrow quays and dockside sheds were no longer appropriate for modern shipping. They were sold by the Mersey Docks & Harbour Company to the Government-appointed Merseyside Development Corporation and were redeveloped using taxpayer's funds.

The Boeing 747's first flight took place on 9 February 1970 and its introduction forever changed the way people travelled, becoming a major factor in the demise of passenger liner services in the 1960s and 1970s, and, together with the development of containerisation, caused a dramatic change in the pattern of cargo services provided by shipping operators around the world. There had been five passenger liners regularly sailing in and out of the Port of Liverpool in 1972. *Empress of Canada* sailed between Liverpool and Quebec until early that year, when she was sold to an American company to cruise out of Miami. Elder Dempster Line's *Aureol* sailed from Liverpool every month on a regular service to West Africa but was transferred to sail out of Southampton in a rationalisation of the service. Shaw Savill Line's *Southern Cross* cruised out of Liverpool in 1970 and 1971, but the company was unable to provide further sailings with the closure of the Liverpool Landing Stage and passenger facilities.

By 1979 the Clan Line's shipping services were operating at a loss. In November 1981 *Clan MacGregor* unloaded at Avonmouth and Manchester's Salford Dock. She was the last Clan Line ship in service and in 1982 became the *Angelika R. Clan MacGillivray*, berthed at Chittagong, was sold at the same time, bringing to an end the history of one of Britain's major shipping lines.

The name of Alfred Holt & Company was changed to Ocean Fleets Limited in 1967 and in 1972 the ships became the responsibility of the various divisions of the Ocean Transport & Trading Company. The company owned the Elder Dempster and Paddy Henderson Lines in 1965, and also acquired the Guinea Gulf Line. The ships were regularly transferred between the different companies during this period and traditional Blue Funnel ships were seen in West African ports.

The company was involved in the creation of Overseas Container Line (OCL), which was taken over by P&O in 1986, and Holt's built several bulk carriers and tankers in 1971–75. They withdrew from the Barber Blue Sea consortium in 1988 and Elder Dempster Line, Palm Line and the Guinea Gulf Line were sold in 1989. When *Memnon* arrived at Falmouth in April 1989 for inspection prior to sale, the Ocean Transport & Trading Company moved out of deep-sea trading to concentrate on offshore operations. In 2000 the Group finally withdrew from owning ships when it sold Cory Towage to the Dutch company Wijsmuller for £81.8 million.

The Ellerman Group was sold for £9 million in 1983 and the remaining ships were registered in the Isle of Man. In 1987 the Line was re-sold to Trafalgar House, who already owned the Cunard Line, and a new freight operation was formed under the name of Cunard-Ellerman with a fleet of nineteen ships. On 14 October 1991, the P&O Steam Navigation Company bought the Ellerman shipping and container interests from Trafalgar House for £42.5 million. Sixteen vessels were involved and Trafalgar House retained the Cunard name. The Mediterranean, Middle East, Indian and East African interests of the Cunard Ellerman Group were also sold to Andrew Weir Shipping Limited (Bank Line).

The Harrison Line purchased *Samaria* and *Scythia* from the Cunard Line in 1969 and they were renamed *Scholar* and *Merchant* respectively. *Benefactor* entered service in 1971 and *Craftsman* followed a year later. A decision to diversify was taken in 1970 and three years later the bulk carriers *Wayfarer*, *Wanderer* and *Warrior* were built in Japan. As the container revolution was changing the face of British shipping, Harrison Line joined with the Hamburg America Line, KNSM and Cie Générale Maritime et Financière in the Caribbean Overseas Line consortium and *Astronomer* was delivered in 1977. The following year CGM joined the consortium, enabling weekly sailings to be provided. Ellerman-Harrison Container Lines provided a service to South Africa.

In 1998 Harrison's share in the joint Ellerman-Harrison service was sold to P&O Nedlloyd, who also acquired the Red Sea/East African liner trade in 1999. On 11 September 2000, P&O Nedlloyd announced that it had bought the liner trading business interests of T. & J. Harrison for the services operated in the European to Caribbean trade and from Europe to the West Coast of South America. The Harrison Line then concentrated on warehousing, transport, airfreight and distribution activities, as well as supplying charts, nautical publications and navigational equipment. Harrison Logistics was established in 2000 as part of the programme of expansion into the customer service and forwarding sector. It was owned by Charente Limited and took the Harrison name into the twenty-first century. However, in early 2002 it was announced that the operation would close as a victim of the recession, marking the end of an era for the Harrison Line.

In 1919 Cunard took over the Brocklebank Line and a service from Calcutta to the United States was introduced. In the 1930s four of their vessels were shortened and experiments were made with motor ships. Following the Second World War, a fleet replenishment programme ensured that the service to Calcutta was able to continue. In 1968 Cunard-Brocklebank Limited was formed and the last Brocklebank ship was delivered. The following years saw the demise of the Brocklebank Line as ships were registered under the Cunard Steamship Company or Cunard-Brocklebank Limited. Ships were transferred from other sectors in the fleet and given Brocklebank names, but by the early 1980s the name had disappeared from the seas.

In 1949 the United Molasses Company Limited (Athel Line) obtained a controlling interest in the Anchor Line and the following year they took over the company completely. In 1955, their centenary year, Anchor Line only owned nine ships and in 1960 a new joint North Atlantic service as introduced under the Anchor-Cunard name. Athel Line became a subsidiary of Tate & Lyle in 1965 and the shares of Anchor Line were reacquired by Runciman's Moor Line Limited. It was then announced that the passenger service to India was to close, with *Circassia* making the last sailing on 13 January 1966. The following years saw Runciman's Moor Line vessels transferred to the Anchor Line and in 1969 the Currie Line was acquired together with their five ships. In the 1970s several bulk carries joined the fleet and in 1976 the company was restructured, with Viscount Runciman retiring as Chairman, a position he had held for thirty years. The following years of that decade saw the sale of most of the Anchor Line vessels, which left them with just the Gibson Line gas tankers.

The Burma Five Star Line was admitted to the Far East Conference in 1959 and the Liverpool-based Bibby Line's share of this trade was halved. However, the charter market was profitable and Bibby ordered three new cargo vessels. In 1965 the passenger service to Colombo and Rangoon was terminated and *Leicestershire* and *Warwickshire* were sold. The former Prince Line vessels *Staffordshire*, *Gloucestershire* and *Herefordshire* maintained the service and two cargo vessels, *Worcestershire* and *Derbyshire*, joined the fleet. Derek J. Bibby joined the board of Charles Hill's Bristol City Line, which gave the line a 22 per cent stake in the company.

The company diversified in the late 1960s and 1970s by entering the liquid petroleum gas carrier market and purchasing motor vehicles and bulk carriers. The war between India and Pakistan had an effect on the trade to those countries, with *Gloucestershire* being sold and the company's longest service closing after over eighty years of operation. By 1978 seven ships out of the fleet of twenty-two were laid up and five ships were mortgaged to finance brokers. However, the company entered the ship management business in 1984 and by 1987 accommodation units, self-elevating jack-up platforms and prison accommodation units were being managed by them. In 1989 the holding company name was changed to Bibby Line Group Limited, though the head office remained in Liverpool. Bibby International Services (IOM) Limited was formed in 1991 and by 1995 this was responsible for managing the Bibby seagoing fleet and the various accommodation and oil industry ventures.

The twenty-year period between 1960 and 1980 was clearly a significant time of change for all those involved in the maritime and shipping industries. The advantages of the carriage of goods in containers were realised and investment was made in new ships, ports and other transport facilities, which were required at the disposal of many conventional vessels and ports. Shipping companies and other maritime agencies that had been operating successfully for over a century needed to amalgamate in order to be able to finance the larger vessels and dock facilities required to operate services. The availability of cheaper air travel was a major factor in the decline of passenger travel by sea, with some shipping operators diversifying by providing cruises with their ships and others moving out of the market completely. Many of the ships mentioned in this book had very short lives and were consigned to the shipbreakers at an early age, while others were sold and converted into cruise ships and became the pioneer vessels of the modern cruise industry.

Empress of Canada, 1961, 27,284 grt. 198 x 26 x 15 m. 20 knots.
b. Vickers-Armstrongs Limited, Newcastle. Yard No. 171. Canadian Pacific Steamships Company.
The *Empress of Canada* is seen leaving her berth and approaching Gladstone Lock. She was built by Vickers-Armstrongs Limited on the Tyne and sailed from Liverpool to Quebec and Montreal via Greenock on 24 April 1961. She was sold to the Carnival Cruise Line in 1972 and was renamed *Mardi Gras*, followed by *Olympic* in 1993, *Star of Texas* in 1994 and *Apollon* in 1996, when she returned to the Mersey for a series of cruises by Direct Cruises. She was sold to the shipbreakers in 2003.

Above: *Empress of England*, 1957, 25,585 grt. 196 x 26 x 15 m. 20 knots.
b. Vickers-Armstrongs Limited, Newcastle. Yard No. 155. Canadian Pacific Steamships Company.
Empress of England was built by Vickers Armstrong at Walker-on-Tyne and sailed on her maiden voyage from Liverpool to Quebec and Montreal on 18 April 1957. In 1962 she broke adrift in Gladstone Dock and collided with the Common Brothers vessel *Hindustan*. In October the following year she was chartered to the Travel Savings Association, making her first cruise for them from Cape Town on the 28th of that month. She returned to Canadian Pacific in April 1965 and resumed working on the Liverpool–Canada service. In April 1970 she was sold to Shaw Savill & Albion, becoming *Ocean Monarch* following an overhaul by Cammell Laird & Company at Birkenhead. She was withdrawn in 1975 and broken up in Kaohsiung.

Below: *Britannic*, 1930, 26,943 grt. 208 x 25 x 16 m. 18 knots.
b. Harland & Wolff Limited, Belfast. Yard No. 807. Cunard Line.
Britannic was built by Harland & Wolff at Belfast. She was launched on 6 August 1929 and sailed on her maiden voyage from Liverpool to New York on 28 June 1930. On 10 May 1934 the Cunard Line and White Star Line amalgamated to become Cunard-White Star Line and *Britannic* made her first voyage from London to New York on 19 April 1935. She was requisitioned by the British Government on 29 August 1939 and operated as a troopship, being attacked by enemy aircraft in the Red Sea in October 1940 and by U-boats in the Atlantic.

She survived the Second World War and returned to the Liverpool to New York service on 22 May 1948. In June 1950 she collided with the American cargo vessel *Pioneer Land* in New York Harbour. Each winter she cruised in the Mediterranean and completed several world cruises with *Caronia*. She suffered a broken crankshaft in 1960 and was briefly laid up at New York. On 25 November 1960 she sailed on her last voyage from New York to Liverpool as the last vessel to sail the North Atlantic in the colours of the White Star Line. *Britannic* was sold to the shipbreakers at Inverkeithing and sailed from Liverpool on 16 December 1960 to be broken up by T. W. Ward.

Caledonia, 1948, 11,252 grt. 154 x 20 x 11 m. 16½ knots.

b. Fairfield Shipbuilding & Engineering Company Limited, Govan. Yard No. 732. Anchor Line.

Caledonia is seen anchored mid-river, waiting to berth at Prince's Landing Stage to load passengers for a voyage to Bombay. She was built in 1948 and completed her service with Anchor Line in 1965, when she became a floating hostel for students at Amsterdam University. She was broken up in Hamburg in 1970.

ANCHOR LINE

INDIA-PAKISTAN
Fares and Information

Cancels all previous issues

Above: *Sylvania*, 1957, 22,017 grt. 185 x 29 x 14 m. 20 knots.
b. John Brown & Company Limited, Clydebank. Yard No. 700. Cunard Line.
Sylvania was built on the Clyde in 1957 and is seen here in Langton Lock in 1967. She replaced *Britannic* on the Liverpool to New York route and in 1965 she made the first Cunard cruise out of Liverpool since 1939. During her overhaul in 1967 she had her hull painted white and was sold to the Sitmar Line in 1968, becoming *Fairwind*. In 1988 she was sold and renamed *Dawn Princess* for Princess Cruises, becoming *Albatros* in 1994. She returned to the Mersey on one occasion while named *Albatros*. She was broken up in Alang in 2004.

Below: *Brescia* (1945/3,834 grt), *Britannic* (1930/26,943 grt) and *Sylvania* (1957/22.017 grt) berthed in Huskisson Dock.

Above: *Empress of England* (1957/25,585 grt) at the company's berth in Gladstone Dock.

Below: Nevasa, 1956, 20,527 grt. 186 x 24 x 15 m. 18 knots.
b. Barclay, Curle & Co., Glasgow. Yard No. 733. British India Steam Navigation Company.
Nevasa was built by Barclay, Curle as a troop transport and was delivered to the British India Line on 12 July 1956. When her troop service ended in 1962 she was laid up in the River Fal and was rebuilt in 1964/65 for use as an educational cruise ship, with accommodation for 307 passengers in cabins and 783 children in dormitories. The British India Line was taken over by the P&O Group in 1972 and *Nevasa* was broken up in Kaohsiung in 1975.

Above: *Reina del Mar*, 20,750 grt. 184 x 24 x 13 m. 18 knots.
b. Harland & Wolff Limited, Belfast. Yard No. 1533. Pacific Steam Navigation Company.
She was launched by Miss Diana Leslie-Bowes on 7 June 1955 and sailed on her maiden voyage from Liverpool to Valparaiso on 3 May the following year. In 1963 she was chartered to the Travel Savings Association and in January 1963 she made her first call at Port Everglades, Florida. Captain Idris Jones, DSC, RD, RNR, was given the freedom of the Port.

In March 1964 she arrived at the builders to be converted to a cruise liner, at 21,501 grt with accommodation for 1,047 passengers in one class. In June she was managed by the Union Castle Line and her first cruise was from Southampton to New York. In November 1964 she was painted in Union Castle Line colours. In 1967 her tonnage became 20,750 grt and was owned by the Royal Mail Line in 1969. In September 1973 she was purchased by the Union Castle Line, and on 30 July 1975 she arrived at Kaohsiung, Taiwan, to be broken up.

Below: *Lady of Mann* (1930/3,104 grt), *Cilicia* (1938/11,136 grt), *Apapa* (1948/11,607 grt) and *Snaefell* (1948/2,489 grt) at Prince's Landing Stage.

Above: *Herculaneum* (1962/161 grt), *Alexandra* (1963/154 grt) and *Apapa* (1948/11,607 grt) at Prince's Landing Stage.

Below: Dunera, 11,197 grt. 158 x 19 x 8 m. 14 knots.
b. Barclay, Curle & Co. Ltd, Glasgow. Yard No. 663. British India Steam Navigation Company. *Dunera* was designed and built as a troop carrier and was launched on 10 May 1937. In 1942 she was converted into an infantry landing ship and served at the Majunga and Sicily landings. She was designated as the headquarters ship of the US Seventh Army for the invasion of Southern France in August 1944. The following year she was employed at Rangoon and later became the lead ship for the Malaysian landings. In 1950–51 she was rebuilt at her builders and was employed carrying troop to Malaya, Ceylon and Cyprus. When the contract for carrying troops ended she was converted into a school cruise ship in 1961, continuing in this role until 1967, when she was withdrawn and broken up in Bilbao.

Above: British India Lines' *Devonia* (1939/12,795 grt).

Below: *Empress of Britain*, 1956, 25,516 grt. 195 x 26 x 15 m. 20 knots.
Canadian Pacific Steamships.
Empress of Britain is seen arriving at Prince's Landing Stage. She was launched by Her Majesty the Queen on 22 June 1955 at the yard of Fairfield Ship Building & Engineering Co. (Yard No. 731) on the Clyde. She sailed from Liverpool to Quebec and Montreal on her maiden voyage on 20 April the following year and was chartered to the Travel Savings Association in 1963. She was then sold to the Greek Line in 1964, becoming *Queen Anna Maria*. She sailed on their transatlantic service until 1975, when she was laid up at Piraeus. In December that year she was sold to the Carnival Cruise Line and became *Carnivale*, before being renamed *Fiesta Marina* in 1994 and later *Olympic*. In 1997 she became *Topaz*, operating as a cruise ship for Thomson Cruise Line, and was then chartered as the Peace Boat until 2008, when she was laid up at Singapore. She was sold to shipbreakers at Alang later that year.

Above: *Empress of England* (1957/25,585 grt) and *Manxman* (1955/2,495 grt) at the Pier Head, Liverpool.

Right: *Mauretania*, 1939, 35,739 grt. 236 x 27 x 18 m. 23 knots.
b. Cammell Laird & Company Limited, Birkenhead. Yard No. 1029. Cunard Line. *Mauretania* in Gladstone Graving Dock in 1963. She was built by Cammell Laird at Birkenhead. She served as a troopship during the Second World War, when she made forty-eight voyages and carried over 355,000 troops. Following her return to service she was employed on transatlantic duties and cruised out of New York in the winter months. She is seen here in 'Caronia' green and was placed on the New York–Cannes–Genoa–Naples service in 1963. She was broken up in Inverkeithing in 1966.

Above: *Remuera*, 1948, 13,619 grt. 162 x 21 x 14 m. 17 knots. b. Harland & Wolff Limited, Belfast. Yard No. 1331. New Zealand Shipping Company. *Remuera* sails on her first voyage for the New Zealand Shipping Company in 1962. She was built for the Cunard Line as *Parthia* and was transferred to the Eastern & Australian Steamship Company in 1965 for the Melbourne to Hong Kong and Japan service while being renamed *Aramac*. She was broken up in 1969.

Above left: The Anchor liner *Cilicia* (1938/11,136 grt) and the Cunard passenger and cargo liner *Media* (1947/13,345 grt) at Prince's Landing Stage on 5 November 1960.

Left: *Kungsholm* (1966/28,891 grt) and *Empress of Canada* (1961/27,284 grt) at the landing stage.

Above: *Aureol*, 1951, 14,083 grt. 164 x 21 x 10 m. 16 knots.
b. Alexander Stephen & Sons Limited, Glasgow. Yard No. 629. Elder Dempster Lines.
Aureol, seen at Brocklebank Dock, Liverpool, was built for Elder Dempster's service from Liverpool to West Africa. Her sister ships on the service were sold by 1968 and *Aureol* made the last West African passenger sailing from Liverpool on 16 March 1972 before being transferred to Southampton. However, she was laid up in 1974 and sold the following year, becoming *Marianna VI* for use as an accommodation ship at Jeddah. She was overhauled at Piraeus in 1979 and berthed at Rabigh in 1980 to operate as an accommodation ship. In 1991 she was laid up off Piraeus and was broken up in Alang ten years later.

Below: *Apapa* (1948/11,607 grt) at the Elder Dempster berth in Brocklebank Dock.

Arkadia, 1931, 20,648 grt. 180 x 26 m. 19½ knots.
b. Vickers-Armstrongs Limited, Newcastle. Yard No. 1. Greek Line.

Owned by Furness Withy for their New York to Hamilton, Bermuda, service, *Arkadia* was built as *Monarch of Bermuda*. She and her sister, *Queen of Bermuda*, left New York at 15.00 on Saturdays, arriving at St George's, Bermuda, at 09.00 on Mondays, with passengers being tendered to Hamilton. They then departed on Wednesday, arriving at New York at 08.00 on Friday. In 1939 she became a troop carrier and operated to Norway, Italy, Portugal and North Africa, and at the end of hostilities she had transported 164,840 personnel and steamed 450,512 miles. On 24 March 1947, while she was being converted back to a passenger vessel, she was almost destroyed by fire.

She was later purchased by the Ministry of Transport and was rebuilt by J. I. Thornycroft as an emigrant carrier, being renamed *New Australia*. She sailed on her first voyage from Southampton to Sydney on 15 August 1950 and was managed by Shaw, Savill & Albion. In 1953 she carried troops to Korea and was sold to the Greek Line in 1958, which resulted in her being refitted by Bloom & Voss at Hamburg and renamed *Arkadia*. Following this refit she was able to carry 150 first class and 1,150 tourist class passengers and sailed on her first voyage for the line from Bremerhaven to Quebec and Montreal on 22 May 1958. Her passenger accommodation was altered again by Bloom & Voss in 1961. Being sold to shipbreakers at Valencia, she arrived there on 18 December 1966.

Above: Elder Dempster's *Apapa* (1948/ 11,607 grt) and *Accra* (1947/11,600 grt) loading cargo at Brocklebank Dock.

Right: *Empress of France*, 1928, 20,123 grt. 177 x 23 x 13 m. 17½ knots.
b. John Brown & Company Limited, Clydebank. Yard No. 518. Canadian Pacific Steamships.
Empress of France was launched as *Duchess of Bedford* on the Clyde on 24 January 1928 by Mrs Baldwin, wife of the British Prime Minister. Her maiden voyage was from Liverpool to Quebec on 1 June that year. In 1939 she was taken over as a troop carrier and sailed on 29 August from Liverpool to Bombay. She was returned to Canadian Pacific in 1947 and arrived at Govan on 3 March to be converted back to a luxury passenger liner. It was initially planned to rename her *Empress of India* but she emerged as *Empress of France* instead, sailing on her first post-war voyage from Liverpool to Quebec and Montreal on 1 September 1948. *Empress of France* was fitted with new streamlined funnels in the winter of 1958/59 and was sold to the British Iron & Steel Corporation at Newport in 1960 and was broken up by J. Cashmore.

Above: *Doulos*, 1914, 6,549 grt. 134 x 18 x 6 m. 14 knots.
b. Newport News Shipbuilding & Dry Dock Company. Yard No. 176. GBA (Good Books for All).
Doulos was originally named *Medina*, when she was owned by the Mallory Steamship Company between 1914 and 1932. In 1932 she was operated by the Clyde Mallory Line and was sold in 1949, becoming *Roma*. She was acquired by Costa Line in 1952 and named *Franca C*. In 1977 she was purchased to operate as a floating bookshop and Christian ministry and was renamed *Doulos*. She continued in this role until 2010, when she was sold to Eric Saw, who renamed her *Doulos Phos*. In 2015 she was hoisted out of the water at Bentan Telani Ferry Terminal to operate as *Doulos Phos the Hotel*.

Above left: British India Lines' educational cruise ship *Uganda* (1952/14,430 grt).

Left: *Carinthia* (1956/21,947 grt) at Prince's Landing Stage.

Above left: *Alsatia*, 1948, 7,226 grt. 153 x 20 x 10 m. 16 knots.
b. J. L. Thompson & Sons Limited, Sunderland. Yard No. 652. Cunard Line.
Completed as *Silverplane* for the Silver Line, and with S. J. Thompson & Co. as managers, both she and her sister *Silverbriar* operated a round-the-world service for their owner. The two vessels were then purchased by Cunard in 1951 to operate on the Liverpool–New York and London–Canada services. On 28 January 1963 the two ships were sold to China Union Lines, Taiwan, and *Alsatia* became *Union Freedom*. She was broken up in Kaohsiung in 1977.

Above right: Cairn Lines' *Cairngowan* (1952/7,503 grt) in the East Float at Birkenhead. She operated as *Manchester Engineer* in 1966, before reverting back to *Cairngowan* the following year. Sold in 1969, she became *Georgilis* and was broken up in 1973.

Below: *Shropshire*, 1959, 7,244 grt. 150 x 19 x 12 m. 17 knots
b. Fairfield Shipbuilding & Engineering Company Limited, Govan. Yard No. 788. Bibby Line.
Shropshire became *Argiro* in 1972, when sold to Lefkonia Cia Naviera SA., and *Naftilos* in 1984. She was broken up in Chittagong in 1985.

Above: *Thistleroy*, 1960, 7,919 grt. 129 x 18 m. 15 knots.
b. J. L. Thompson & Sons Limited. Yard No. 244. Albyn Line Limited – Allan, Black & Company Limited, Sunderland.
She became *Ingleton* in 1966, when owned by the Somerston Shipping Company (Chapman & Willan Limited), *Panetolikon* when owned by Neptunea Mundial of Monrovia in 1970 and *Shabaan* when belonging to Askeladd Shipping Corporation of Panama in 1981. In 1981 she was acquired by Najd Maritime Transport Company of Saudi Arabia and retained her name. On 19 November 1983 she was damaged in a collision in the Karnaphuli River, and was broken up in 1984 at Chittagong.

Below: *Devon City*, 1960, 10,300 grt. 155 x 20 m. 14½ knots.
b. William Doxford & Company Limited, Pallion. Yard No. 838. Sir William Reardon Smith & Sons Limited.
Devon City in Alfred Dock, Birkenhead. She became *Executive Venture* in 1972, *Tong Beng* in 1974, *Pentay* in 1978 and was broken up in 1986.

Above: *Alaunia*, 1960, 7,004 grt. 150 x 19 x 8 m. 17½ knots.
b. William Hamilton & Company Limited, Port Glasgow. Yard No. 522. Cunard Line.
In 1969 she was transferred to Cunard-Brocklebank and renamed *Malancha*. She was sold with her sister in 1971, becoming *Humi Nasita*, and was then renamed *Yungming* in 1973 and *Hong Qi 108* in 1975. She was deleted from the register in 1993.

Above right: Booth Line's *Anselm* (1950/10,946 grt) in the Mersey.

Right: *Letitia* (1961/4,667 grt) was owned by the Donaldson Line.

23

Above: *Ivernia* (1964/5,586 grt) and *Parthia* (1963/5,586 grt) in Huskisson Dock, Liverpool. *Ivernia* became *Manipur* in 1970, then *Concordia Manipur* and *Manipur* again in 1971, followed by *Philippa* in 1977. She was later broken up in Chittagong in 1985. *Parthia* was sold in 1971, becoming *Wambiri* and *Staship 1*, and then *Rice Trader* in 1979. On 27 January 1984 her engine failed off Socotra and she was towed to Djibouti. She left in tow for Karachi on 4 April and was broken up in Gadani Beach.

Below: *Media*, 1947, 13,345 grt. 162 x 21 x 14 m. 17 knots.
b. John Redhead & Company, South Shields. Yard No. 629. Cunard Line.
Media was the first new vessel built for the Cunard Line following the Second World War, sailing on her maiden voyage from Liverpool to New York on 20 August 1947. She was fitted with stabilisers in 1952 when her promenade deck was glazed. *Media* and her sister ship *Parthia* were dual cargo-passenger vessels and it became uneconomical to operate them. Her last passenger sailing for the Cunard Line was in September 1961 from Liverpool to Quebec and Montreal. She was sold to Cogeder Line, Genoa, in 1961 and was modernised and rebuilt by Officine A&R Navi at Genoa, becoming *Flavia*, and was able to accommodate 1,224 passengers in one class. *Flavia* was initially employed on the Genoa–Australia route and later on the Bremerhaven–Southampton–Australia route. In 1968 she was cruising in the Mediterranean with winter cruises in the Caribbean. In 1969 she was sold to Costa Armatori S.p.A of Naples and cruised out of Miami. She was sold to Flavian Shipping SA., Panama, was renamed *Flavian* and was laid up at Hong Kong in 1982. In 1986 she was purchased by Lavia Shipping of Panama, renamed *Lavia* and was again laid up at Hong Kong. On 7 January 1989 she suffered a serious fire and was beached and declared a total loss.

CUNARD	Gross Tons	PORT LINE	Gross Tons	THOS. & JNO. BROCKLEBANK	Gross Tons
Queen Elizabeth	83,673	Port New Plymouth	13,085	Maipura	9,748
Queen Mary	81,237	Port Auckland	11,945	Manaar	8,970
Mauretania	35,655	Port Brisbane	11,942	Matra	8,954
Caronia	34,172	Port Napier	11,834	Mahseer	8,945
Sylvania	21,989	Port Hobart	11,149	Mangla	8,805
Carinthia	21,947	Port Wellington	10,588	Mathura	8,782
Ivernia	21,717	Port Pirie	10,535	Makrana	8,767
Saxonia	21,637	Port Vindex	10,480	Mawana	8,744
Parthia	13,362	Port Melbourne	10,470	Masirah	8,733
Media	13,345	Port Victor	10,409	Manipur	8,569
Asia	8,723	Port Sydney	9,992	Maidan	8,566
Arabia	8,720	Port Phillip	9,947	Mahronda	8,537
Assyria	8,683	Port Jackson	9,827	Mahanada	8,489
Andria	7,228	Port Launceston	8,957	Magdapur	8,488
Alsatia	7,226	Port Nelson	8,950	Malancha	8,288
Andania	7,004	Port Invercargill	8,847	Macharda	8,117
Alaunia	7,004	Port Chalmers	8,717	Marwarri	8,091
Brescia	3,841	Port Wyndham	8,702	Malakand	8,078
Lycia	3,534	Port Townsville	8,681	Matheran	8,051
Phrygia	3,534	Port Huon	8,524	Martand	8,007
Pavia	3,411	Port Alma	8,419	Maihar	7,684
		Port Fairy	8,406	Maturata	7,365
	417,642	Port Adelaide	8,114	Maskeliya	7,350
		Port Dunedin	7,585	Makalla	7,190
		Port Lyttelton	7,413	Mandasor	7,067
		Port Macquarie	7,329		
		Port Lincoln	7,253		208,385
		Port Montreal	7,179		
		Port Quebec	6,777		
		Port Halifax	5,925		
		Port Saint John	5,911		
		Crusader	834		
		(3,337) 16/64the			
		Saracen	835		
		(3,341) 16/64the			
			285,561		

	Ships on order				
	No. 1630 Port Alfred	9,600	No. 678		8,700
	No. 1631	9,600			
	No. 1646	13,000			
		32,200			8,700

Total Gross Registered Tonnage of Cunard and Subsidiary Companies Existing Fleets 911,588

Total Gross Tonnage on order 40,900

Cunard and subsidiary companies' fleets in 1960.

Cunard Freight Service

Cunard M.V. Media, 7,300 tons

Liverpool to New York Direct

	Receiving Cargo				Sails	Estimated Arr.
SCYTHIA (R)	Jan. 20	to	Jan. 26		Jan. 28	Feb. 5
RIKKE SKOU	Jan. 27	to	Feb. 2		Feb. 4	Feb. 12
ALAUNIA (R)	Feb. 3	to	Feb. 9		Feb. 11	Feb. 19
MEDIA (R)	Feb. 10	to	Feb. 16		Feb. 18	Feb. 26
SAMARIA (R)	Feb. 17	to	Feb. 23		Feb. 25	Mar. 5
IVERNIA (R)	Feb. 24	to	Mar. 2		Mar. 4	Mar. 12
SCYTHIA (R)	Mar. 3	to	Mar. 9		Mar. 11	Mar. 19

Liverpool to Boston, Hampton Roads, Baltimore and Philadelphia (via New York)

SCYTHIA (R) (Omits Hampton Roads)	Jan. 20	to	Jan. 25		Jan. 28	Feb. 11 (Boston)
RIKKE SKOU (Omits Boston)	Jan. 27	to	Feb. 1		Feb. 4	Feb. 18 (Hampton Roads)
ALAUNIA (R) (Omits Hampton Roads)	Feb. 3	to	Feb. 8		Feb. 11	Feb. 25 (Boston)
MEDIA (R) (Omits Boston)	Feb. 10	to	Feb. 15		Feb. 18	Mar. 4 (Hampton Roads)
SAMARIA (R) (Omits Hampton Roads)	Feb. 17	to	Feb. 22		Feb. 25	Mar. 11 (Boston)
IVERNIA (R) (Omits Boston)	Feb. 24	to	Mar. 1		Mar. 4	Mar. 18 (Hampton Roads)
SCYTHIA (R) (Omits Hampton Roads)	Mar. 3	to	Mar. 8		Mar. 11	Mar. 25 (Boston)

Liverpool to Halifax N.S. & St. John N.B.

BONITA	Jan. 26	to	Feb. 2		Feb. 4	Feb. 14 (Halifax)
LANCASTRIAN	Feb. 9	to	Feb. 16		Feb. 18	Feb. 28 (Halifax)
ANDRIA	Feb. 22	to	Mar. 2		Mar. 4	Mar. 14 (Halifax)

Liverpool to Mobile, Houston, Galveston and New Orleans

ANTONIA	Feb. 24	to	Mar. 4		Mar. 7	Mar. 21 (Mobile)

(R) REFRIGERATED SPACE   LOADING BERTH : HUSKISSON DOCK

Bills of Lading must be presented by Shippers or Agents not later than the day after vessel's closing date.

No. 82   SUBJECT TO CHANGE WITHOUT NOTICE

C491 24/1/66
P.T.O.   Printed in England

Cunard's Freight Service sailing list for 1966.

Above: *Parthia* (1963/5,586 grt),
Sylvania (1957/22,017 grt) and
Ivernia (1964/5,586 grt) in
Huskisson Dock.

Left: *American Traveler*, 1946,
8,228 grt. 140 x 19 m. 16 knots.
b. North Carolina Shipbuilding Co.,
Wilmington. Yard No. 237. United
States Lines.
She was sold and renamed
Amercrest in 1969 before being
broken up in Kaohsiung, where she
arrived on 9 April 1972.

Above: *Tangistan*, 1950, 7,383 grt. 145 x 18 m. 12½ knots.
b. John Readhead & Company, South Shields. Yard No. 567. Strick Line.
Tangistan arrived at Kaohsiung on 13 March 1972 and was broken up.

Below: *Laertes*, 1950, 7,664 grt. 141 x 19 x 9 m. 15½ knots.
b. Vickers-Armstrongs Limited, Newcastle. Yard No. 112. Blue Funnel Line.
Sister of *Calchas*, she was delivered in October 1950 as the final Mark A2 Class vessel and was managed by NSM Oceaan. She was transferred to Blue Funnel in 1972, becoming *Idomeneus*, and was operated by Elder Dempster in 1975. Sold to Gulf Shipping Lines the following year, she became *Gulf Voyager*, and arrived at Gadani Beach on 8 May 1978 to be broken up.

Above: *Machaon*, 1959, 8,529 grt. 139 x 20 x 11 m. 16½ knots.
b. Caledon Ship Building & Engineering Company, Dundee. Yard No. 515. Blue Funnel Line. A Menelaus Class ship, she was handed over to the Ocean Steamship Company and transferred to NSM Oceaan in 1975, then to Elder Dempster Lines two years later, becoming *Obuasi*. The following year she was sold to Thenamaris Maritime Incorporated of Piraeus, becoming *Elsea*, and then to Tartan Shipping Limited of Monrovia, becoming *Med Endeavour*. She was broken up in Kaohsiung in 1979.

Below: *Neleus*, 1953, 7,802 grt. 149 x 20 x 9 m. 16 knots.
b. Caledon Ship Building & Engineering Company, Dundee. Yard No. 486. Blue Funnel Line. A Nestor Class ship, she sailed on her maiden voyage on 21 March 1953 and was sold to Akamas Shipping Company, Cyprus, in 1971, becoming *Aegis Fable* and then *Aegis Trust* the following year, when she was owned by Alikarnassos Shipping Company. She left Niigata in Japan on 17 March 1974 to be broken up in Shanghai.

Above: *Annoula II*, 1960, 8,509 grt. 139 x 20 x 11 m. 16½ knots.
b. Vickers-Armstrongs Limited, Newcastle. Yard No. 167. Blue Funnel Line.
A Menelaus Class ship, she was built as *Melampus*. On 6 June 1967 she was trapped in the Suez Canal during the Six-Day War between Israel and Egypt. Sold to the underwriters in 1971, she was then sold on to the Grecomar Shipping Agency Limited. On 20 May 1975 she was towed to Trieste, and following an overhaul she was sold to the Korissianev Shipping Company SA., becoming *Annoula II*. Fourteen ships were trapped in the canal and only *Munsterland* and *Norwind* were able to leave under their own power. *Annoula II* was broken up in Gadani Beach in 1983.

Below: *Woodarra*, 1957, 8,753 grt. 159 x 21 x 13 m. 17½ knots.
b. Barclay, Curle & Co., Glasgow. Yard No. 737. British India Line.
She was launched on 22 November 1956 and became *Pando Gulf* in 1968, operating on the P&O Far East service. She was transferred to the Cargo Division of P&O in 1971 and was sold to the Ben Line three years later, becoming *Benalbanach*. She arrived at Inchon on 21 May 1978 and was broken up.

Above left: *Maskeliya*, 1954, 7,350 grt. 144 x 18 x 8 m. 15 knots.
b. William Hamilton & Company Limited, Port Glasgow. Yard No. 496. Brocklebank Line.
She was the first Brocklebank vessel to be fitted with bi-pod masts and air conditioning in the crew quarters. In 1963 she made one voyage for the Guinea Gulf Line to West Africa. In 1968 she was transferred to Cunard-Brocklebank Limited and was placed for sale on the market. The following year she was sold to Ocean Shipping & Enterprises SA., Panama, becoming *Ocean Joy*, and was broken up in Kaohsiung in 1972.

Above right: *Manipur*, 1945, 8,559 grt. 154 x 19 x 10 m. 14 knots.
b. William Hamilton & Company Limited, Port Glasgow. Yard No. 461. Brocklebank Line.
Delivered in December 1945, *Manipur* was built to wartime restrictions before being modernised two years later. In December 1960 she suffered a major engine malfunction and was sold for breaking up in 1966, arriving at Whampoa on 6 January 1967.

Shaftsbury, 1958, 8,532 grt. 139 x 19 x 9 m. 14 knots.
b. Burntisland Ship Building Company, Burntisland. Yard No. 382. Houlder Brothers.
Completed for the Alexander Shipping Company, with Houlder Brothers & Company as managers, *Shaftsbury* was acquired by First United Carriers Incorporated of Panama (Del Bene Ultramar SA. Group) in 1972 and renamed *Portloe*. She became *Arauco* the following year and was then sold to Cia Chilena de Navegación Interoceánica of Valparaiso. In 1978 she was renamed *Jal Sea Condor* for the Fife Shipping Company of Panama. On 3 July 1978, on a voyage from Bangkok to Lagos, she developed a leak off Walvis Bay and was abandoned. Her crew was taken on board the Russian fish factory ship *Schilute* and she was taken in tow, bound for Walvis Bay. However, she sank three days later, on 6 July.

Ikeja Palm, 1961,
5,682 grt. 160 x 22 m.
15 knots.
b. Swan, Hunter &
Wigham Richardson
Limited, Walker. Yard
No. 1982. Palm Line
Limited.
She became *GME Palma*
in 1981 and then *Palma*
in 1982, before arriving
at Gadani Beach on
24 November the
following year to be
broken up.

The West Float at
Birkenhead in 1972.

Cock tugs assist
the ore carrier *Sir
Andrew Duncan*
(1958/10,687 grt) into
the north lock at Alfred
Dock, Birkenhead. She
became *Filia* in 1973
and suffered serious
engine damage off
Ghana on 2 April 1979.
She arrived at Bilbao
on 31 December that
year and was broken
up by Recuperaciones
Submarinas.

(SEE OVER)

HARRISON LINE

WEST COAST PORTS to West Indies, Venezuela, Colombia (Atlantic Ports). Cristobal (for Panama and Central American destinations), Jamaica, Mexico (Atlantic) and Belize

ALL CARGO TAKEN BY SPECIAL AGREEMENT ONLY

For Barbados, Trinidad, La Guaira, Puerto Cabello, Curacao and Maracaibo

DIPLOMAT †	Receiving **Liverpool:** for Venezuelan ports **17th December/6th January** for other ports **20th December/10th January** Scheduled to sail 13th January. † *Omits Maracaibo*
CROFTER	Receiving **Liverpool:** for Venezuelan ports **7th/20th January** for other ports **11th/24th January** Scheduled to sail 27th January.
CRAFTSMAN	Receiving **Liverpool:** for Venezuelan ports **21st January/3rd February** for other ports **21st January/7th February** Scheduled to sail 10th February.

Cargo for Ciudad Bolivar, Guiria, Carupano, Guanta, Cumana, Pampatar and Las Piedras will be accepted on through bills of lading via Puerto Cabello and for Aruba via Curacao.

Cargo for Antigua, Dominica, Grenada, Montserrat, St. Kitts, St. Lucia, St. Vincent and Tobago will be accepted on through bills of lading via Trinidad.

For Kingston, Vera Cruz and Tampico
Alternate vessels calling at Belize

DEFENDER	Receiving **Liverpool: 4th/17th January** Scheduled to sail 20th January.
WANDERER	Receiving **Liverpool: 18th/31st January** Scheduled to sail 3rd February. Calls Belize
ADVENTURER	Receiving **Liverpool: 1st/14th February** Scheduled to sail 17th February.

For Cristobal (for Colon, Panama, Balboa, Port-au-Prince, and West Coast of Central America)

PACIFIC STRONGHOLD	Receiving **9 Shed, 8 Dock, Salford: 2nd/10th Jan. 8 Princes Dock, Glasgow: 11th/14th Jan.** Scheduled to sail from Glasgow 20th January.

Liverpool Loading Berth : EAST SIDE BRUNSWICK DOCK, unless otherwise stated.

Through rates of freight from Hull, Glasgow, Leith and Bristol Channel Ports may be had on application (*West Indies and Demerara excepted*).

Deck Cargo, Hazardous Cargo, Lock-up Stowage Cargo and Pieces or Packages exceeding 5 tons weight will be accepted only by special arrangement and delivery date agreed

Liverpool, 5th January, 1961.

Above left: The ore carrier *Knightsgarth* (1961/10,591 grt) preparing to dock at the West Float, Birkenhead. She became *Theoskepasti* in 1975 and was broken up in Aliaga in 1986.

Above right: Harrison Line's *Trader* (1966/6,488 grt) and *Statesman* (1964/6,162 grt) in the River Mersey. *Trader* was sold in 1980, becoming *Bangpa-In*, and left Kobe on 23 December 1983 on her final voyage. She was broken up in Rayong in 1986. *Statesman* was sold to Ocean Tramping Company of Hong Kong in 1977, becoming *Jiang Chang*. On 11 November 1990 she foundered 70 miles north-east of Vietnam on a voyage from Singapore to Hainan Island.

Left: Harrison Line's sailing list.

Above left and right: Harrison Line's *Linguist* (1966/6,162 grt) loading cargo. She was sold with *Trader* (1966/6,488 grt) in 1980 and was renamed *Bangplee*. The following year she became *Unisol* and on 7 December 1983 she broke her moorings during a gale at Chandler, on the Gulf of St Lawrence, and was wrecked.

Below: Advocate (1963/8,604 grt) on charter to T. & J. Harrison in Canada Dock, Liverpool. She was built for the Asiatic Steam Navigation Company as *Nurjehan*. The company was formed in 1878 under the auspices of the Liverpool merchant house Turner & Company and their Calcutta associates, Turner Morrison & Company. The ships were cross-traders, serving the coastal trade between Calcutta and Bombay, between Calcutta, Chittagong, Rangoon and Moulmein, and later between Calcutta and Java via Malayan ports. Asiatic also acquired the Indian Government mail contract between Calcutta and the Andaman Islands, which included responsibility for the transport of convicts to the penal colony at Port Blair.

In 1912 the British India Steam Navigation Company and Asiatic joined forces to acquire the Bombay & Persia Steam Navigation Company (later the Mogul Line, which was a leading carrier of Muslims on pilgrimages). Following a rate war, in the 1930s the Indian national line Scindia was invited to join the two companies. However, British India became the dominant partner and soon took over Asiatic. Asiatic and Mogul later became part of the P&O Group. Mogul was sold to Indian interests in 1960, and British India acquired the remaining Asiatic shares the following year. In 1965 management of Asiatic's vessels passed to P&O's tramp management company Hain Nourse, and by 1977 the Asiatic Steam Navigation Company was renamed P&O Bulk Shipping Limited. *Nurjehan* was chartered to T. & J. Harrison in 1972 and renamed *Advocate*. She reverted back to *Nurjehan* the following year before becoming *Strathnevis* in 1975. She was then sold to Unimed Shipping Company in 1978 and was renamed *Ioannis*, and then *Dimitrios P. Papastratis* in 1982. She was broken up in 1984.

Above left: Harrison Line's *Wayfarer* (1951/8,150 grt) was sold in 1971 and renamed *Mitera Zafira*. On 28 March 1973 she ran aground on fire outside Constanza and was abandoned, becoming a constructive total loss.

Above right: *Factor*, 1948, 6,533 grt. 141 x 17 x 9 m. 14 knots.
b. Chas Connell & Company, Glasgow. Yard No. 456. Harrison Line.
On 26 July 1951 she sustained severe bottom damage when she was grounded on the Rio Magdalena Bar, Colombia. She arrived at Bilbao on 21 March 1972 and was broken up.

Below: *Journalist*, 1954, 8,366 grt. 141 x 18 x 10 m. 13½ knots.
b. William Doxford & Sons, Sunderland. Yard No. 801. Harrison Line.
Journalist is seen here loading cargo in the West Float at Birkenhead. In May 1973 she was sold to the Neptune Shipping Company of Cyprus and was renamed *Aghia Thalassini*. In 1977 she was owned by Lamyra Cia Naviera SA. of Piraeus, retaining the same name. She was later sold to Greek and Lebanese interests in 1981, becoming *Elissar*, and was broken up at Gadani Beach the following year.

Above left: *Explorer*, 1961, 7,200 grt. 134 x 18 x 9 m. 15½ knots.
b. Nederland Dok & Schps Werke, Amsterdam. Yard No. 490. Harrison Line.
She was acquired by Cia Macedonia de Nav. SA. of Greece in 1979 and renamed *Link Trust*. The following year she was owned by Senator Maritime Incorporated, Greece, and ran aground at the mouth of the Calabar River on 12 December on a voyage from Antwerp to Calabar. She was floated two weeks later and entered the port to discharge her cargo. In 1981 she was sold to Greek interests, becoming *Baru Spirit*, and was broken up in China in 1985.

Above right: *Magician*, 1968, 8,454 grt. 151 x 19 x 8 m. 18 knots.
b. William Doxford & Sons Ltd., Sunderland. Yard No. 884. Harrison Line.
In July 1979 she was damaged by a serious fire in the galley at La Guaira, Venezuela. Renamed *Cherry Crystal* in 1981, she arrived at Alang on 19 June 1985 to be broken up.

Harrison Line's *Author* (1959/8,715 grt) in the Mersey channel.

Above: *Naturalist*, 1965, 6,162 grt. 124 x 17 x 8 m. 16 knots.
b. A/B Lindholmens Varv., Gothenburg. Yard No. 1091. Harrison Line.
In 1977 *Naturalist* was sold to the People's Republic of China, Canton, was renamed *Yi Chang* and was broken up in China in 1991.

Below: *Wanderer*, 1951, 4,525 grt. 140 x 18 x 10 m. 12 knots.
b. William Doxford & Sons Limited, Sunderland. Yard No. 790. Harrison Line.
Wanderer is pictured unloading cargo in the south dock system at Liverpool. In July 1958 she collided with the dredger *Mersey No. 27* in the River Mersey. She was sold to Tricia Shipping Company of Nicosia in October 1970 and was renamed *Cleopatra*. Acquired by Chung Lien Nav. Co. of Panama in 1974, she became *Chung Thai* before being broken up in South Korea later that year.

Above left: *Tactician*, 1962, 8,844 grt. 149 x 19 x 9 m. 16 knots.
b. William Doxford & Sons Limited, Sunderland. Yard No. 845. Harrison Line.
In October 1962 *Tactician* was berthed at Belize during a hurricane and provided assistance to the town in the form of communications, medicines and food until relief ships arrived. On 4 July 1968 she suffered an engine room fire and was towed into Ponta Delgada by the *Rapallo*. Two members of her crew lost their lives in an engine room explosion in August 1972, and she put in to Walvis Bay for repairs. Sold to Cypriot interests in 1979, she was renamed *Sea Luck*. In October 1980 she became *Kero* and was broken up in Peru in 1987.

Above right: *Craftsman*, 1972, 6,721 grt. 162 x 22 x 9 m. 18 knots.
b. Doxford & Sunderland Limited, Sunderland. Yard No. 900. Harrison Line.
Seen here loading at the Harrison Line berth in the West Float at Birkenhead, *Craftsman* had a relatively short life with the company as she was sold to the Ierax Shipping Company of Greece and renamed *Forum Craftsman* in 1981. Sold again to Marigold Navigation Company in 1987, she was then laid up, before becoming *Regal Crusader* in 1988 and *Christina J* in 1992. On 18 August 1994 she arrived at Cebu and was broken up.

Below: *Clan Alpine*, 1966, 8,713 grt. 155 x 19 x 11 m. 16 knots.
b. Greenock Dockyard/Scotts Shipbuilding & Engineering Company, Greenock. Yard No. 708. Clan Line.
Clan Alpine in Alfred Dock, Birkenhead. While she was under construction at the Greenock Dockyard the shipyard went into liquidation and she was completed by Scotts. She was the Clan Line's final ship and held the same name as the company's first vessel. In 1981 she was sold to Delibra Shipping Company of Monrovia and was renamed *African Diamond*, becoming *African Amber* the following year. On 2 May 1984 she arrived at Kaohsiung and was broken up.

Above left: *Clan Chattan*, 1943, 9,585 grt. 149 x 19 x 12 m. 15 knots.
b. Greenock Dockyard Company, Greenock. Yard No. 456. Clan Line.
On a voyage from London to Hull in September 1950, *Clan Chattan* grounded 3 miles north of the Sunk lightship and was re-floated with damage to her bottom. In January 1962 she was transferred to the King Line and arrived at Hong Kong on 14 May to be broken up.

Above right: *Clan Matheson*, 1957, 7,685 grt. 153 x 21 x 8 m. 16 knots.
b. Greenock Dockyard Company, Greenock. Yard No. 489. Clan Line.
Clan Matheson is seen loading cargo at the Clan Line berth in Vittoria Dock, Birkenhead. She arrived at Kaohsiung on 12 December 1978 and was broken up.

Below: Clan Line sailing list for 1961.

CLAN LINE

TO
LOBITO - SOUTH & SOUTH EAST AFRICA   MAURITIUS

CAYZER, IRVINE & CO., LTD.,
LONDON - 2 ST. MARY AXE, E.C.3 - Tel. AVE 2010

Liverpool - Royal Liver Building, Tel. Maritime 2040   Glasgow - 109 Hope Street, Tel. CEN. 7050.

VESSEL	GLASGOW (King George V. Dock) Receiving	GLASGOW Closing	NEWPORT (Alexandra Dock) Closing	BIRKENHEAD (Vittoria Dock) Receiving	BIRKENHEAD Closing	Sailing B'head	DISCHARGE PORTS
m.v. TANTALLON CASTLE	—	—	—	Now (For Mauri)	15 Aug. tius Closin	19 Aug. g 11 Aug.)	LOBITO, WALVIS BAY, CAPETOWN, MOSSEL BAY, PORT ELIZABETH, EAST LONDON, MAURITIUS
m.v. CLAN MACDONALD	Now	21 Aug.	—	21 Aug. (For Beira)	29 Aug. Closing	2 Sep. 25th Aug.)	DURBAN, LOURENCO MARQUES, BEIRA •
† m.v. CLAN MACINDOE (Substituted for CLAN MACTAGGART)	23 Aug.	31 Aug.	—	31 Aug. (For Beira)	8 Sep. Closing	13 Sep. 6th Sep.)	DURBAN, LOURENCO MARQUES, BEIRA •
m.v. STIRLINGSHIRE	—	—	‡ 2 Sep.	2 Sep. (For Beira)	12 Sep. Closing	16 Sep. 8th Sept.)	TENERIFFE, CAPETOWN, PORT ELIZABETH, EAST LONDON, DURBAN, LOURENCO MARQUES, BEIRA •
† t.s.s. CLAN MACLENNAN	31 Aug.	14 Sep.	—	14 Sep.	22 Sep.	27 Sep.	LOBITO, CAPETOWN, MOSSEL BAY, PORT ELIZABETH, EAST LONDON, MAURITIUS
† m.v. CLAN MACILWRAITH	7 Sep.	21 Sep.	—	21 Sep. (For Beira)	29 Sep. Closing	4 Oct. 25th Sep.)	DURBAN, LOURENCO MARQUES, BEIRA •
t.s.s. CLAN DAVIDSON	26 Sep.	2 Oct.	—	2 Oct.	10 Oct.	14 Oct.	DURBAN, LOURENCO MARQUES, BEIRA •
† m.v. CLAN FRASER (MAIDEN VOYAGE)	21 Sep.	5 Oct.	—	5 Oct.	13 Oct.	18 Oct.	LOBITO, CAPETOWN, PT. ELIZABETH, EAST LONDON, MAURITIUS

‡ Subject to Inducement

• Cargo for BEIRA must be specially booked before despatch.

Through Bills of Lading issued to

WALVIS BAY, } With Transhipment at   INHAMBANE, CHINDE, QUELIMANE, MACUSE, MOMA, } With Transhipment at
LUDERITZ BAY } CAPETOWN.   ANTONIO INES, MOZAMBIQUE, NACALA, PORT AMELIA. } LOURENCO MARQUES

Vessels have liberty to call at other U.K. Ports and at other ports either on or out of route.
All Cargo carried by Special Agreement only and subject to all terms, conditions
and exceptions of Shipping notes, wharfingers' receipts and Bills of Lading.
† Cool Chamber and Refrigerator cargo can be accepted by arrangement.
Goods Insured on the most favourable Terms.
· Special accommodation for Livestock
Sailings are subject to alteration or cancellation without notice.

Above left: Clan Line's *Clan Alpine* (1966/8,713 grt) and the Blue Funnel cargo vessel *Priam* (1966/12,094 grt) in Vittoria Dock, Birkenhead.

Above right: *Clan Maclaren* (1946/6,389 grt) and *Protesilaus* (1967/12,094 grt).

Below: *Argyllshire*, 1956, 9,299 grt. 163 x 21 x 9 m. 16¾ knots.
b. Greenock Dockyard Company, Greenock. Yard No. 486. Clan Line.
Argyllshire was designed for the Australian meat and wool trade as the company's longest ship. In 1960 she was transferred to the Scottish Shire Line, with Turnbull, Martin as managers. Sold to the Gulf East Marine Limited of Monrovia in 1975, she was renamed *Schivago*. She arrived at Kaohsiung on 3 August 1977 and was broken up.

Above: *Clan Mackinnon*, 1945, 137 x 17 x 11 m. 12 knots.

b. John Redhead & Sons Limited, South Shields. Yard No. 1177. Clan Line.

Launched on 10 July 1945 as *Empire Dunnet* for the Ministry of War Transport, with Cayzer Irvine & Company as managers, she was purchased by Clan Line in 1946 and renamed *Clan Mackinnon*. In 1955 she was transferred to the British & South American Steam Navigation Company, with Houston Line as managers. She was chartered to the Sri Lankan Navy in 1958 to transport 600 Tamil separatists to Jaffna and return a group of Ceylonese to Colombo. In 1961 she was sold to Mullion & Company, Hong Kong, becoming *Ardross*. She was renamed *Labuan Bay* in 1963 and broken up in Kaohsiung in 1967.

Below left: Clan Line sailing list for the maiden voyage of *Clan Macilwraith* from Glasgow and Birkenhead in 1961.

Below right: Clan Line vessels unloading at Alexandra Dock, Liverpool.

King Henry, 1957,
5,993 grt. 142 x 18 x 9 m.
12½ knots.
b. Harland & Wolff
Limited, Belfast. Yard
No. 1587. King Line.
She was transferred to
Clan Line in 1959 and
Houston Line in 1970.
Sold to A. Marcopoulos
of Piraeus in 1972, she
became *African Lady*
and then *African Lion*
two years later. She was
broken up in 1983.

Khuzistan, 1955,
7,145 grt. 146 x 18 m.
13 knots.
b. John Redhead & Sons
Limited, South Shields.
Yard No. 580. Strick Line.
She became *Foochow* in
1973 and was broken up
in Whampoa in 1977.

Cumberland, 1948,
11,272 grt. 170 x 21 x
10 m. 17 knots.
b. John Brown &
Company Limited,
Clydebank. Yard No. 614.
Federal Line.
Cumberland became
part of P&O's General
Cargo Division in
1971 and transferred
to P&O ownership
two years later. She
arrived at Kaohsiung on
25 December 1976 and
was broken up.

An advertisement for the New Zealand Shipping Company and the Federal Steam Navigation Company for 1966.

A Hall Line/Harrison Line joint service advertisement for 1961.

Above: *City of Bath*, 1947, 7,030 grt. 147 x 19 x 9 m. 15½ knots.
Built as *Langleeclyde* for the Medomsley Steam Shipping Company by the Blythswood Ship Building Company (Yard No. 85), she was purchased by Ellerman Lines in 1952, becoming *City of Bath*. In 1969 she was sold to the Constantinos Shipping Company of Famagusta and was renamed *Lena*. On 22 March 1972 she arrived at Castellon from St John, New Brunswick, and was broken up.

Below: *City of Glasgow*, 1963, 10,017 grt. 155 x 20 x 9 m.
b. Vickers-Armstrongs Limited, Newcastle. Yard No. 173. Ellerman Bucknall Line.
Renamed *City of Ottawa* in 1971 for the Canadian service, she was later acquired by Y. C. Cheng's Pacific International Lines (Pte) in 1978, being renamed *Kota Cahaya* for their Singapore–Persian Gulf service, which she worked with with *Kota Cantik* (ex-*City of Eastbourne*/*City of Toronto*). She was broken up in China in 1985.

43

City of Carlisle, 1946,
9,913 grt. 152 x 20 x 12 m.
14½ knots.
b. Cammell Laird &
Company Limited,
Birkenhead. Yard No. 1156.
Ellerman & Bucknall Line.
Sold to Waywiser
Navigation Corporation,
Keelung, in 1963, she
was renamed *Jeannie*
before being broken up in
Kaohsiung in 1970.

City of New York, 1947,
8,420 grt. 152 x 20 x 10 m.
14 knots.
b. Vickers-Armstrongs
Limited, Newcastle. Yard
No. 97. Ellerman Hall Line.
She was sold to
Mardevoto Cia Nav. SA.,
Greece, in 1967, becoming
Kavo Matapas. She was
broken up in Kaohsiung
two years later.

City of Leeds, 1950,
7,622 grt. 148 x 19 x 9 m.
14 knots.
b. Vickers-Armstrongs
Limited, Newcastle. Yard
No. 114. Ellerman Hall
Line.
Laid down as *City of
Guildford*, she was delivered
as *City of Ottawa* for
the Hall Line. She was
renamed *City of Leeds* in
1971 and was sold to Gulf
(Ship-Owners) Limited,
London, in 1976, becoming
Gulf Venture. She was
broken up in Gadani Beach
in 1977.

City of Glasgow, 1958,
4,954 grt. 132 x 18 x 8 m.
14½ knots.
b. Robb, Caledon Limited,
Dundee. Yard No. 514.
Ellerman Hall Line.
Delivered as *City of
Hereford,* she was
renamed *City of Glasgow*
in 1971. She was sold
to the Porter Shipping
Company in 1978,
becoming *Myrna*, before
being broken up in
Kaohsiung in 1980.

City of Canberra, 1961,
10,306 grt. 156 x 21 x 9 m.
18 knots.
b. Barclay, Curle & Co.,
Glasgow. Yard No. 747.
Ellerman & Bucknall
Line.
Transferred to Ellerman
City Lines in 1973, she
was sold to Tasman
Gold Shipping Limited
of Singapore in 1978,
becoming *Tasgold*.
She was broken up in
Kaohsiung in 1980.

City of Hull, 1947,
8,458 grt. 152 x 20 x 10 m.
14 knots.
b. Vickers-Armstrongs
Limited, Newcastle. Yard
No. 98. Ellerman Hall
Line.
Sold to Embajada Cia
Nav. of Panama in 1967,
she was renamed *Essex*
and broken up in Japan.

45

Above left: *Tung Lee*, 1943, 8,459 grt. 150 x 20 x 10 m.
b. Swan, Hunter & Wigham Richardson Limited, Newcastle. Yard No. 1661. Far Eastern Navigation Corporation.
Delivered as *City of Bristol* to Ellerman City Line, she was later acquired by the Far Eastern Navigation Corporation in 1961 and renamed *Tung Lee*. She was broken up in 1964.

Above right: The West Float at Birkenhead.

Below: *Island of Marmara*, 1960, 6,980 grt. 132 x 18 x 8 m. 14¾ knots.
On a voyage from Calcutta to Chalna during the Pakistani civil war in November 1971, she was attacked by a gunboat and hit forty-nine times; fortunately there were no casualties and she returned to Calcutta for repairs. In June 1977 she was part of the Queen's Silver Jubilee review on the Mersey. She was sold to the Venture Investment Trust of Piraeus in 1979, becoming *Island of Marmara*. On her first voyage for the company she collided with Everard's *Conformity* in St George's Channel and was towed to Swansea. She was broken up in 1983 at Jamnagar.

Above: City of Philadelphia, 1949, 7,591 grt. 148 x 19 x 9 m. 14 knots.

b. Furness Ship Building Company, Haverton Hill, Stockton-on-Tees. Yard No. 423. Ellerman Hall Line.

She was laid down as *City of Cardiff*, and entered service as *City of Philadelphia*. Acquired by Marbrava Cia Nav. SA., Piraeus, in 1971, she became *Kaptaspyro* and then *Spyro* in 1970 for the Spyros Shipping Company of Famagusta. She was broken up the following year at Whampoa.

Below left: Federal Steam Navigation Company vessels loading cargo at Gladstone Dock, Liverpool.

Below right: Booker Line's *Booker Venture* (1961/9,516 grt), Elder Dempster's *Dunkwa* (1960/6,109 grt) and Harrison Line's *Explorer* (1961/7,200 grt) in Canada Dock, Liverpool.

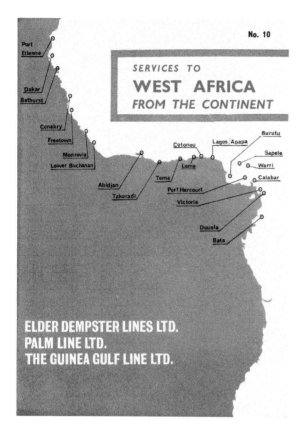

SERVICES TO
WEST AFRICA
FROM THE CONTINENT

Port Etienne
Dakar
Bathurst
Conakry
Freetown
Monrovia
Lower Buchanan
Abidjan
Takoradi
Tema
Lome
Cotonou
Lagos / Apapa
Burutu
Sapele
Warri
Calabar
Port Harcourt
Victoria
Douala
Bata

ELDER DEMPSTER LINES LTD.
PALM LINE LTD.
THE GUINEA GULF LINE LTD.

Left: A 1963 map of Elder Dempster, Palm Line and Guinea Gulf Line services to West Africa.

Below: *Donga*, 1960, 6,565 grt. 142 x 19 x 8 m. 14 knots.
b. Lithgows Limited, Port Glasgow. Yard No. 1133. Elder Dempster Lines. Launched on 12 April 1960 for the British & Burmese Steam Navigation Company, and chartered to Elder Dempster Lines. In 1964 she was transferred to Elder Dempster ownership. On 26 March 1981 she was acquired by Diamant Merchant Shipping Limited, becoming *Diamant Merchant*. Following a change of ownership to Cyprus interests in 1983 she was renamed *Lydra* and was broken up later that year.

Above: *Dunkwa*, 1960, 6,109 grt. 140 x 19 x 8 m. 14 knots.
b. Scotts Shipbuilding & Engineering Company Limited, Greenock. Yard No. 685. Elder Dempster Lines.
Dunkwa was laid up at Liverpool in 1980 and was sold to the Clare Shipping Corporation, Piraeus, the following year, being renamed *Clare*. On her first voyage she suffered engine damage in Rio de Janeiro and was declared a total loss. Sold to Resolve Maritime Limited of Panama, she was renamed *Resolve*, and was broken up in 1983 at Gadani Beach by Elahi Shipbreakers.

Below: *Boniface* (1979/3,636 grt) and *Benedict* (1979/3,636 grt), seen laid up in Vittoria Dock, Birkenhead. A four-ship order was made with Engenharia de Máquinas SA. of Rio de Janeiro, with two ships intended for the Liverpool service and two for routes out of New York. However, the New York service was becoming uneconomical and the order was reduced to two ships. *Boniface* left Heysham on Booth's final voyage on 24 April 1986 and the two ships were laid up at Vittoria Dock, Birkenhead. They were sold to Lošinjska Plovidba-Brodarstvo of Croatia, with *Benedict* becoming *Zamet*, then *Ismail Prince* in 2005, *Ramiah II* in 2010 and *Nawal II* in 2011, while *Boniface* was renamed *Pecine*, then *Seven Star* in 2005, *Reef Mahe* in 2006 and *Obs Swathy* in 2007. *Boniface* was broken up in 2009 and *Benedict* at Mumbai in 2011.

BOOTH ⊠ LINE

EXPRESS MAIL VESSELS

R.M.S. "DUNSTAN"

RECEIVING
1st FEBRUARY to 15th FEBRUARY
AT S.W. 2 QUEENS DOCK.

SAILING FROM LIVERPOOL
17th FEBRUARY, 1961

FOR

BARBADOS TRINIDAD
BELÉM AND MANAUS

REFRIGERATOR SPACE AVAILABLE

CARGO ALSO CARRIED ON TRANSHIPMENT BASIS TO
ANTIGUA, DOMINICA, GRENADA, MONTSERRAT, NEVIS, ST. KITTS,
ST. LUCIA, ST. VINCENT, TOBAGO, BOLIVIA, LETICIA and IQUITOS.

Following vessel—R.M.S. "DENIS" receiving 1st to 15th MARCH

For further particulars apply to:—
THE BOOTH STEAMSHIP CO. LTD., Cunard Building, Liverpool 3
Telephone No. CENtral 9181
25th January, 1961   FOR AREA AGENTS IN U.K. SEE OVERLEAF

Left: Booth Line sailing list for 1961.

Below: *Baltistan*, 1953, 7,489 grt. 147 x 18 m. 13½ knots. b. Readheads, South Shields. Yard No. 573. Strick Line. She is seen leaving the Manchester Ship Canal at Eastham, heading to Liverpool to load cargo for a voyage to the Persian Gulf. She became *Elindia* in 1972 and *Gulf Diamond* the following year. On 20 May 1974 she was wrecked and was broken up in Gadani Beach later that year.

Above: *Bardic*, 1950, 8,827 grt. 144 x 19 x 11 m. 14 knots.
b. Vickers-Armstrongs Limited, Newcastle. Yard No. 116. Bibby Line.
Delivered as *Eastern Prince*, she was chartered to Shaw, Savill & Albion in 1960 and renamed *Bardic*. Acquired with *Cingalese Prince* by the Bibby Line in 1964, she was then renamed *Staffordshire*. On a voyage from Liverpool to Rangoon on 30 November 1970 she diverted to Colombo with engine problems. It was decided that she was uneconomic to repair and so she was towed to Hong Kong to be broken up by Fuji Marden & Company.

Below left: *Pizarro*, 1955, 8,494 grt. 156 x 20 x 9 m. 16 knots.
b. Greenock Dockyard Company, Greenock. Yard No. 485. Pacific Steam Navigation Company Limited.
She was sold to Navieros Progresivos SA., Piraeus, and renamed *Kavo Maleas*. She was later broken up in Kaohsiung in 1974.

Below right: *Amaralina*, 1970, 10,192 grt. 161 x 23 m.
b. Gdańska Lenina, Gdańsk. Yard No. b444/01. Empresa de Nav. Aliança SA.
She became *Forum Eagle* in 1983 and was broken up in Xingang in 1985.

Velarde, 1957,
2,055 grt. 102 x 14m
15½ knots.
b. Ottensen,
Hamburg.
Yard No. 502.
MacAndrews Line.
Velarde became
Sailor Prince in
1969, *Zenit* in 1970
and *Nadir* in 1973,
and arrived at
Split on 27 April
1987, where she
was broken up.

MacAndrew Line
advertisement
for 1969.

Tropic,
ex-*Nova Scotia*
(1975/6,660 grt), in
Huskisson Dock.

Palm Line's *Elmina Palm* (1957/5,356 grt) leaving Liverpool.

Work commenced in the early 1960s on the new Royal Seaforth Container Terminal. To enable container traffic to pass through the port, a temporary terminal was provided when Gladstone Graving Dock was converted into a wet dock. The graving dock was completed in 1913, before the rest of the dock became operational. It is 320 metres long and 37 metres wide and was designed to take the largest transatlantic steamers at the time.

Atlantic Cinderella, 1970, 15,437 grt. 197 x 28 m. 23 knots. b. Dunkerque et Bordeaux, Dunkirk. Yard No. 270. Atlantic Container Line (Wallenius Rederierna).
Arriving at Kaohsiung on 19 January 1986, she was broken up by Chi Shun Hua Steel Corporation.

Sheaf Wear, 1959, 10,867 grt. 154 x 21 m. 12 knots. b. Laing & Sons, Deptford Yard. Yard No. 821. W. A. Souter & Company Ltd (Sheaf Steam Shipping Company Ltd). *Sheaf Wear* became *Baltic Ore* in 1969, *Irish Wasa* in 1971 and *Christina* in 1977. She arrived at Bilbao on 18 April 1977 and was broken up.

Dapo Trader, 1961, 13,082 grt. 160 x 21 m. 12 knots. b. Pickersgill & Sons, Southwick. Yard No. 367. Cia Evpo SA. She was built as *Cheviot*, becoming *Dapo Trader* in 1977 and then *Trader* in 1984. She arrived at Setúbal on 1 July 1984 and was broken up.

Hemimactra, 1956, 12,278 grt. 170 x 21 m. 14½ knots. b. Cammell Laird & Company Limited, Birkenhead. Yard No. 1241. Shell Bermuda (Overseas) Limited. Delivered as *San Fortunato*, she became *Hemimactra* in 1964. She then arrived at Kaohsiung on 10 February 1977 and was broken up by Chin Tai Steel Enterprise Company.

World Friendship, 1965, 47,344 grt. 265 x 37 m. 16½ knots.
b. Atlantique, Saint-Nazaire. Yard No. Q22. Niarchos Group.
She was broken up in Kaohsiung in 1978 by Ching Steel Enterprise Company.

British Gunner, 1954, 10,076 grt. 157 x 20 m. 12½ knots.
b. Harland & Wolff Limited, Govan. Yard No. 1466. BP Tanker Company Limited.
She became *Clyde Gunner* in 1961, before reverting back to *British Gunner* in 1963. She arrived at Vinaroz on 17 May 1972 and was broken up by Desguaces Maritime SA.

British Mallard, 1960, 11,174 grt. 160 x 21 m. 15 knots.
b. Harland & Wolff Limited, Belfast. Yard No. 1588. B. P. Tanker Company Limited.
She became *Penhors* in 1978, *Fal XII* in 1984 and *Fame 2* in 1987.
She arrived at Gadani Beach on 8 July 1987 and was broken up by G. N. Brothers.

Morar, 1959, 6,990 grt. 130 x 18 m. 11 knots. b. Lithgows Limited, Port Glasgow. Yard No. 1113. Scottish Ore Carriers Limited. She was sold in 1967 and renamed *Clari*, followed by *Arnis* in 1969 and *Mahoni* in 1974. On 26 September 1979 she was grounded off Taiwan and was broken up in Kaohsiung the following year.

Athelcrest, 1957, 7,548 grt. 140 x 19 m. 14½ knots. b. Lithgows Limited, Port Glasgow. Yard No. 1096. Athel Line. *Athelcrest* was sold and became *Maori* in 1971 and *Al Salimi V* in 1979. She was broken up at Gadani Beach in 1980.

Irish Holly, 1954, 2,940 grt. 101 x 14 m. 14 knots. b. Grays, Hartlepool. Yard No. 1279. Irish Shipping Limited. She became *Etnea* in 1967 and was wrecked near Vibo Valentia on 7 January 1968. She was then broken up in La Spezia, where she arrived on 12 June 1968.

Drupa, 1966, 39,795 grt. 244 x 34 m. 16 knots. b. Deutsche Werft, Finkenwerder. Yard No. 780. Shell Tankers Limited. She arrived at Alang on 20 April 1993 and was broken up.

Eucadia, 1946, 7,005 grt. 152 x 20 m. 15 knots. b. Barclay, Curle & Co., Glasgow. Yard No. 704. Anchor Line. She was sold in 1963, becoming *Ionian* and later *Macedon*. On a voyage from Houston to Bombay she was wrecked at Pigeon Rocks, near Beirut, and was broken into three parts.

Sprayville, 1920, 466 grt. 46 x 8 m. b. Cochrane & Sons Limited, Selby. Yard No. 746. John S. Monks Limited. Built as *Pickmere*, she became *Sprayville* in 1931. She arrived at Barrow on 20 June 1958 and was broken up by T. W. Ward.

Leicestershire, 1948, 8,908 grt. 146 x 18 x 10 m. 15½ knots. b. Fairfield Shipbuilding & Engineering Company, Govan. Yard No. 745. Bibby Line. Sold in 1965, she was renamed *Heraklion*. On 8 December 1966 she capsized on a voyage from Canea to Piraeus. Out of the 281 people on board, only forty-seven survived.

Makrana, 1957, 8,764 grt. 151 x 19 m. 16½ knots. William Hamilton & Company Limited, Port Glasgow. Yard No. 515. Brocklebank Line. She was sold in 1971, becoming *Aegis Glory* and later *Aegis Eternity*. On 23 April 1974 she was stranded and damaged off Singapore, being broken up later in Shanghai, where she arrived in June of that year.

Union Castle Line's *Kinnard Castle* (1956/7,681 grt) and the Blue Funnel vessel *Idomeneus* (1950/7,664 grt) in Alfred Dock, Birkenhead.

Elder Dempster's *Fian* (1963/7,689 grt) and the Pacific Steam Navigation Company's *Pizarro* (1955/8,564 grt) in Huskisson Dock, Liverpool.

Jag Laxmi, 1957, 8,800 grt. 149 x 19 m. b. Hitachi, Sakurajima. Yard No. 3789. Great Eastern Shipping Company Limited. In 1976 she became *Jag Vani* and later *Kedarnath*. She was wrecked on a voyage from Calcutta to Singapore on 7 June 1980.

Indian Shipper, 1944, 7,612 grt. 139 x 19 m. 16 knots. b. California Shipbuilding Corporation. Yard No. V4. India Steamship Company. Built as *United States Victory*, she became *Indian Shipper* in 1947. She arrived at Kaohsiung on 26 April 1971 and was broken up by Yih Ho Steel & Iron Company Limited.

Indian Exporter, 1945, 7,604 grt. 139 x 19 m. 16 knots.
b. Oregon Shipbuilding Company, Portland. Yard No. 1233. India Steamship Company.
Built as *Temple Victory*, she became *Indian Exporter* in 1947 and *Samudra Usha* in 1972. She arrived at Bombay on 8 August 1977 and was broken up by the Akbarali Steel Syndicate.

Safmarine and Indian Steamship Company vessels unloading cargo at Langton Dock, Liverpool.

India Steamship Company and Furness Withy Group advertisements for 1969.

Right: J. Lauritzen Lines' advertisement for services from Liverpool to Quebec in December 1960.

Below: The Compañía Sud Americana de Vapores (CSAV) sailing list for 1966.

Nordholm, 1958,
7,061 grt. 139 x 18 m.
b. A/S Nakskov SV,
Skibsværft, Nakskov.
Yard No. 149. DNK
Copenhagen.
She became *Gorgo* in
1974 and then *Gorgona*
in 1985, and was broken
up in Sachana in 1985.

Atlantic Ocean, 1962,
9,292 grt. 151 x 19 x 11 m.
16 knots.
b. Swan, Hunter &
Wigham Richardson,
Wallsend. Yard No. 1933.
Tat On Shipping,
Mogadishu.
Built as *Clan Finlay*
for the Clan Line, she
became *Arya Far* in 1968
and *Atlantic Ocean* in
1971. Acquired by the
China Ocean Shipping
Company in 1975, she
was renamed *Lu Chan*
before being broken up
in China in 1992.

Suruga Maru, 1957,
9,564 grt. 155 x 20 m.
17½ knots.
b. Mitsubishi, Yokohama.
Yard No. 819. Nippon
Yusen Kaisha.
Renamed *Tokelau*
in 1975, she arrived
at Kaohsiung on
24 February 1978 to
be broken up.

Above: Sinyeh, 1953, 10,783 grt. 162 x 21 m.
b. P. Smith, Rotterdam. Yard No. 604. Ocean Tramping Company Limited.
She was built as *Karimata*, becoming *Sinyeh* in 1972. On 27 December 1975 she suffered a serious fire and was beached off Latakia, where she was later broken up.

Below: Tian Men, 1974, 10,058 grt. 152 x 20 m. 18 knots.
b. Warnowwerft Warnemünde, Rostock. Yard No. 386. Qingdao Ocean Marine.
Tian Men was a member of the 'Ozean' class, with thirty-five units being built from 1970 to 1980. The ships were designed as multi-purpose freight vessels built for the transport of containers, general cargo, heavy goods, industrial equipment and bulk cargo in temperate and tropical zones. There were five variants of the class and ten went to the People's Republic of China, seven to Norway, four each to France and Romania, three to Croatia and the Netherlands and one each to Argentina, India, Madagascar and the Czech Republic. *Tian Men* became *Yu Qiang* in 1992 and was deleted from the register on 18 June 2012.

Above: *Marianthe*, 1970, 7,093 grt. 153 x 22 x 8 m. 18¼ knots.
b. Robb Caledon Shipbuilders Limited, Dundee. Yard No. 554. Sun Horizon Naviera SA. (Diana Shipping Agencies).
Built as *City of Liverpool*, she became *Marianthe* in 1981. On 25 November 1985 she was grounded off Turk's Head and was re-floated on 4 December. She arrived at Kaohsiung on 16 September 1986 and was broken up.

Below: *Logos*, 1949, 2,319 grt. 82 x 13 m.
b. Helsingør Værft, *Denmark*. Yard No. 290. Educational Books Exhibits Limited.
Built as *Umanak*, she became *Logos* in 1971 and was wrecked on 5 January 1988.

Tove Maersk, 1954,
8,456 grt. 146 x 19 m.
b. Boelwerf, Temse. Yard
No. 1306.
Tove Maersk became
Equatorial in 1967 and
was broken up in La
Spezia in 1975.

River Ogun, 1968,
7,827 grt. 137 x 19 m.
b. Rheinstahl Nordsee,
Emden. Yard No. 397.
Nigerian National Line.
She was sold and
renamed *Shogun,* then
Fairview in 1984 and
Fame the following year.
She was broken up in
Gadani Beach in 1985.

Arya Man, 1961,
9,292 grt. 151 x 19 m.
16 knots.
b. Swan, Hunter &
Wigham Richardson,
Wallsend. Yard No. 1919.
Arya National Shipping
Lines, SA.
Built as *Clan Forbes*, she
became *Arya Man* in 1968
and *Iran Hemmet* in 1980.
She was broken up in
Alang in 1985.

Above: *Safina-e-Rehmat*, 1958, 8,595 grt. 135 x 19 m.
b. Tirreno. Yard No. 239r. Pakistan Shipping Corporation.
She was originally named *Frederico Parodi*, becoming *Safina-e-Rehmat* in 1965. She was broken up at Gadani Beach in 1993.

Below: *Pussar*, 1965, 8,798 grt. 152 x 19 m. 18 knots.
b. Bartram & Sons, South Dock. Yard No. 404. Pakistan National Shipping Corporation.
Pussar was broken up at Gadani Beach in 1984.

Above: *Mona's Isle* (1951/2,491 grt) is assisted into Alfred Dock, Birkenhead, by the Alexandra tug *Egerton* (1965/172 grt).

Below: *Manx Maid* (1962/2,724 grt) and *Snaefell* (1948/2,489 grt) in the River Mersey off the Pier Head.

Otto Thoresen's *Viking II* at Prince's Landing Stage on 27 October 1964. She also visited Avonmouth, Southampton, Hull, Newcastle and Leith and was built to operate from Southampton to Cherbourg and Le Havre. She was named Car Ferry *Viking II* in 1964, became *Earl William* in 1977, *Pearl William* in 1992, *Mar Julia* in 1996, *Cesme Stern* in 1997, *Windward II* in 2000 and *Ocean Pearl* in 2006. She became a hotel in Chaguaramas, Trinidad and Tobago, in 2008. On 2 April 2011 she was under tow from Chaguaramas to Venezuela by the tug *Icon 1* when the tug collided with the drill ship *Petrosaudi Saturn*. The collision caused the drill ship to move and the well was lost, with an estimated loss of $100 million. It was reported that this was Lloyd's second largest loss in 2011. Following the collision, *Ocean Pearl* sank.

Above: *Leinster*, 1948, 4,115 grt. 112 x 15 m. 17½ knots.
b. Harland & Wolff, Belfast. Yard No. 1352. British & Irish Steam Packet Limited.
She was sold, becoming *Leinster 1* in 1968 and *Aphrodite* the following year. She arrived
at Aliaga on 11 October 1987 to be broken up.

Below: *Munster*, 1948, 4,115 grt. 112 x 15 m. 17½ knots.
b. Harland & Wolff, Belfast. Yard No. 1349. British & Irish Steam Packet.
In 1968 she was renamed *Munster I*, and when sold to the Epirotiki Steamship Navigation
Company (George Potamianos SA., Piraeus, Greece) later that year she became *Theseus*.
She was renamed *Orpheus* in 1969 and operated for Royal Olympic Cruises Limited. She
arrived at Alang on 28 December 2000 and was broken up.

The Isle of Man
Steam Packet
vessels *King Orry*
(1946/2,485 grt)
and *Tynwald*
(1947/2,487 grt) in
Bidston Graving
Dock. The dock is
no longer used as a
dry dock.

The Isle of
Man steamer
Lady of Mann
(1930/3,014 grt) at
Cavendish Wharf,
Birkenhead.

The Isle of Man
steamer *Manxman*
(1955/2,495 grt)
approaching
Liverpool
Landing Stage.

Tynwald
(1947/2,487 grt).

Lady of Mann
(1976/2,990 grt)
leaving Liverpool.

Duke of Rothesay
(1956/4,780 grt)
arriving at Langton
Dock for her annual
overhaul in Liverpool.

Above: *Munster*, 1968, 4,067 grt. 110.2 x 18.1 m.
b. Nobiskrug, Rendsburg. Yard No. 657. British & Irish Steam Packet Company Limited.
She was introduced in 1968 on the Liverpool–Dublin service as the route's first roll-on/roll-off car ferry. In 1983 she was sold, becoming *Farah* and *Farah 1* and then *Tian Peng* in 1990. She was broken up in China in 2002.

Below: Leinster, 1969, 4,849 grt. 118.3 x 17.8 m.
b. Verolme Dockyard, Cork. Yard No. 9/800. British & Irish Steam Packet Company Limited.
She was launched on 19 November 1968 for the Dublin–Liverpool car ferry and passenger service. In 1980 she was renamed *Innisfallen*, then *Ionian Sun* in 1986, *Chams* in 1993, *Ionian Sun* again in 1994 and then *Merdif* in 2001. She was broken up in Sachana in 2004.

Above: *Bardic Ferry*, 1957, 2,550 grt. 103 x 17 m. 14 knots.
b. William Denny & Brothers, Dumbarton. Yard No. 1489. Atlantic Steam Navigation Company Limited. She became *Nasim II* in 1976 and was broken up in Aliaga in 1988.

Right: *Orwell Star (1)/Orwell*, 1956, 495 grt. 53 x 9 m.
b. Bijlholt, Foxhol. Yard No. 555. Blue Star Line.
She was removed from the register in 2012.

Escaut (1,947/399 grt) in the south dock system at Liverpool.

Hannes Knuppel, 1967, 499 grt. 68 x 11 m. b. Sietas, Neuenfelde. Yard No. 587. Anna & Hans Knüppel. She became *Kora* in 1971, *Mylinda* in 1993 and *Caytrans Caribe* in 1995, before foundering on 27 May 1998.

Tuskar (1962/1,115 grt) leaving Waterloo Dock for Waterford.

Above: *Dundalk*, 1939, 699 grt. 56.69 x 10.66 x 3.96 m.
b. Ardrossan Dockyard Limited, Ardrossan. Yard No. 372. British & Irish Steam Packet Company.
Launched as *Dundalk* on 10 November 1938. In 1939 she was delivered to the British & Irish Steam Packet Company Limited in Dublin before later being sold to Varverakis & Company, Greece, in 1966 and renamed *Alexis*. On 5 September that year, on a voyage from Constantza to Beirut with a cargo of sheep and eggs, she sank 35 miles west of Paphos, Cyprus.

Below: *Audacity*, 1968, 699 grt. 72.6 x 11.1 m.
b. George Brown & Company Limited, Greenock. Yard No. 225. F. T. Everard & Sons Limited.
Launched as *Empire Audrey* on 22 February 1943, she was acquired by F. T. Everard in 1946 and renamed *Audacity*. She arrived at Boom in August 1967 and was broken up following damage by grounding.

The British & Irish Steam Packet's *Wicklow* (1938/586 grt).

F. T. Everard & Sons' *Authenticity* (1947/861 grt) in Alfred Dock, Birkenhead.

Imperial Chemical Industries' *Calcium* (1959/644 grt)

Above: *Wirral Coast*, 1962, 881 grt. 62 x 10.9 x 4.93 m. 12½ knots.
b. Cammell Laird & Company Limited, Birkenhead. Yard No. 1308. Coast Lines.
On a voyage from Ireland to Liverpool on 8 November 1969, *Wirral Coast* lost two containers in gale force winds and was towed to Birkenhead, where part of her cargo was discharged at the West Float. Sold to James Tyrrell Limited in 1972, she was renamed *Shevrell*, before later being purchased by Usborne & Son Limited (with Buries Markes Limited as managers) in 1973, becoming *Portmarnock*. In 1978 she was owned by Fulpass Limited (with G. T. Gillie & Blair Limited as managers). It was announced that she would be renamed *Brookline* but this did not occur and she remained as *Portmarnock*. Sold to Khodor Itani, Lebanon, in 1979, she was renamed *Nadia 1* before being re-sold to Mrs Nadia Hussein Mekkaoui, also of Lebanon, and being renamed *Nadia*. She was wrecked off the coast of Lebanon in a storm on 27 November 1985. (Photo: Dave Crolley Collection)

Below: The Isle of Man Steam Packet Company cargo vessel *Peveril* (1964/1,048 grt).

The British &
Irish Steam
Packet Company's
container terminal at
Trafalgar Dock.

The passenger
terminal at
Trafalgar Dock.

The Alexandra
Towing Company
tug *Brockenhurst*
(1964/174 grt) being
lifted out of the water
by the Mersey Docks
& Harbour Board's
floating crane *Samson*
following her sinking
in 1984.

Above: *Brocklebank* (1965/142 grt) off Alfred Dock, Birkenhead.

Below: J. H. Lamey Limited advertisement for 1960.

J. H. LAMEY LTD.

Telephone : Cent. 6411/2   703 TOWER BUILDINGS, LIVERPOOL, 3   Telegrams : " Lamey Liverpool 3 "

Tugs fitted with Radio Telephone, V.H.F. and Radar Equipment

Tugs :
Alfred Lamey
Anita Lamey
B. C. Lamey
Edith Lamey
Irene Lamey
J. H. Lamey
James Lamey
John Lamey
Margaret Lamey
Marie Lamey
William Lamey

FOR TOWAGE ON THE MERSEY

Above: *Marie Lamey* (1940/161 grt) in the Mersey. She was broken up in Troon in 1967.

Below: *William Lamey* (1959/166 grt) became *Wapping* in 1970, *Theodorus 1* in 1985, *Agios Rafail* in 2002, *Fox 1* in 2003 and *Andreas L* in 2008.

J. H. Lamey (1964/216 grt) was renamed *Hornby* when Lamey was taken over by the Alexandra Towing Company in 1970. She was sold to operate in Northern Ireland in 1984 and her name was changed to *Samuel F.*

North Cock (1903/149 grt) was built by Laird Brothers Limited at Birkenhead (Yard No. 656) for the Liverpool Screw Towing & Lighterage Company and was demolished at Liverpool in 1964.

Above: Alexandra Towing Company's *Salthouse* (1935/192 grt) off Alfred Dock, Birkenhead.

Left: *Hazelgarth* (1959/230 grt) and *Marie Lamey* (1940/161 grt) in dry dock.

Right: Lamey, Rea and Alexandra tugs at Liverpool.

Below: Alexandra, Furness and Rea tugs awaiting orders at Liverpool.

Above: *Willowgarth* (1959/230 grt) and *Minegarth* (1922/179 grt) in the West Float, Birkenhead. *Minegarth* was broken up in Troon in 1964 and *Willowgarth* became *Thisseas* in 1986 and then *Capetan Giannis* in 1988.

Below: Liverpool Lighterage Company Limited's *Langbourne* (1913/63 grt) off the Liverpool Landing Stage.

Above: J. H. Lamey's *Irene Lamey* (1915/192 grt). She was broken up in Preston in 1964.

Below: The Birkenhead ferry *Claughton* was built in 1930 and survived until 1962, when she was withdrawn and broken up.

Above: The Birkenhead Corporation ferry *Woodchurch* (1960/464 grt).

Below: *Overchurch* (1962/468 grt) on the Woodside–Liverpool (Pier Head) service.

Above: Passengers prepare to board the Birkenhead ferry at Liverpool Landing Stage. The Wallasey ferry *Leasowe* (1951/567 grt) arrives from Seacombe and the Cunard passenger liner *Parthia* (1948/13,362 grt) embarks passengers for a voyage to New York.

Below: *Woodchurch* (1960/464 grt) and *Egremont* (1952/566 grt) laid up in Morpeth Dock, Birkenhead.

Above: Mersey Docks & Harbour Board dredger *Mersey No. 26* (1948/1,363 grt) working in the river off Langton Dock. She was sold in 1974, becoming *Triaena*, and was broken up in Gijon later that year.

Below: *Mersey No. 27* (1949/387 grt). She was sold in 1974 and broken up in San Esteban de Pravia.

A Ferguson Brothers advertisement.

Imperial Chemical Industries'
Cuddington (1948/201 grt).

Cooper's *P. M. Cooper* and *John L. K.*
in dock at Liverpool.

Mersey Docks & Harbour Board's floating crane *Titan* (1952/665 grt) was sold in 1974 and broken up in San Esteban de Pravia.

A rainbow over the Four Bridges road in the 1960s.

Mancunium (1946/1,378 grt).

Above: The pilot vessel *Sir Thomas Brocklebank*. She was sold and renamed *Odysseus* in 1977, and was broken up in Vejle in 1982.

Below: The Mersey Docks & Harbour Board buoy maintenance and survey vessel *Aestus* (1950/95 grt). She was sold to shipbreakers in 1986.

Above: *Poilo* (1921/307 grt) was a small oil tanker designed to deliver fuel directly to vessels, and was owned by Shell-Mex & BP Limited. She was re-engined in 1951 and arrived at Troon on 17 August 1967 to be broken up.

Below: The Royal Yacht *Britannia* berthed at the Liverpool Landing Stage for a visit by Her Majesty the Queen to Merseyside.

Rea tugs in Alfred Lock, preparing to position a drilling rig off Gladstone Dock to enable survey work to be carried out prior to work commencing on the new Seaforth Dock.

The floating crane *Mammoth* (1920/1,524 grt). She was sold in 1987.

Engineers working on the large cranes at the iron ore berth at Bidston Dock.

Rea shunting engines at Bidston Dock.

Above: HNLMS *De Ruyter* (C801) was completed for the Royal Netherlands Navy in 1953 and was acquired by the Peruvian Navy in 1973, serving as the fleet flagship *Almirante Grau* (CLM-81). She completed a major overhaul between 1985 and 1988, when she was fitted with new weapons and electronics. She was decommissioned on 26 September 2017.

Below: *Sir Bedivere* (L3004) was a Landing Ship Logistic and saw service in the Falklands War, the Persian Gulf and Sierra Leone. She was decommissioned on 18 February 2008 and was sold to the Brazilian Navy, becoming *Almirante Saboia* (G-25).

Above: HMS *Ulster* was a U class destroyer that was commissioned on 30 June 1943. She was later converted into a Type 15 anti-submarine frigate with the pennant number F83. She was used for training in the Sonar Control Room in the 1960s, and later as a training hulk at HMS *Raleigh*. She was broken up in 1980.

Below: HMS *Albion* was commissioned on 26 May 1954. She is pictured arriving at Prince's Landing Stage on a visit to the port, when she was open to the public. In 1973 she was sold for conversion into a heavy-lift vessel for North Sea oil exploration. However, the plans did not materialise and she was broken up in Faslane.